Praising God in the Valley

Lessons and Other Blessings in the Journey through Cancer

JOYCE HERR

WESTBOW
P R E S S®
A DIVISION OF THOMAS NELSON
& ZONDERVAN

This book is a work of non-fiction. Unless otherwise noted, the author and the publisher make no explicit guarantees as to the accuracy of the information contained in this book and in some cases, names of people and places have been altered to protect their privacy.

WestBow Press books may be ordered through booksellers or by contacting:

WestBow Press
A Division of Thomas Nelson & Zondervan
1663 Liberty Drive
Bloomington, IN 47403
www.westbowpress.com
844-714-3454

Scripture marked (KJV) taken from the King James Version of the Bible.

Scripture marked (NKJV) taken from the New King James Version®. Copyright © 1982 by Thomas Nelson. Used by permission. All rights reserved.

Scripture quotations marked (TLB) are taken from The Living Bible copyright © 1971. Used by permission of Tyndale House Publishers, a Division of Tyndale House Ministries, Carol Stream, Illinois 60188. All rights reserved.

ISBN: 978-1-6642-1664-8 (sc)
ISBN: 978-1-6642-1665-5 (e)

Library of Congress Control Number: 2020924821

Print information available on the last page.

WestBow Press rev. date: 01/11/2021

This book is dedicated to all those fellow travelers
who are walking through the valley.

My prayer is that God will use this book to bring you
encouragement, hope and peace in your journey through cancer.

With gratitude to:

All my family and friends who supported me
with their love, encouragement, help
and prayers during my ongoing journey through cancer.

My daughter-in-law Carrie, my daughter Cathleen, and my
granddaughter Rachel and her husband Matthew, who stayed
with me and cared for me when I was unable to care for myself.

My daughter Laura who provided lots
of TLC, encouragement, and
especially for her companionship mixed in with a
delightful spirit of fun on treatment days.

My niece, Joyce Howard, an oncology nurse
and instructor, who patiently
answered many of my questions about cancer, and
provided invaluable insight and advice.

To my wonderful friend, Kim McAinsh
who persistently encouraged and
prayed for me in the process of writing this book.

The team of volunteers from my church, Harvest
New Beginnings Church in Oswego, Illinois
for providing meals during my weeks of treatment.

"My Sister and Me Ministries" for a wonderful care gift package.

The "Prayer Shawl Ministry" of Faith Lutheran
Church of Arlington Heights, Illinois
for a beautiful crocheted prayer shawl.

Most of all, I want to thank my dear Lord and Savior Jesus Christ
for His abiding presence and unfailing love, strength,
and hope as I walk through this valley.

Contents

Introduction

For your love and kindness are better to me than life itself.
How I praise You! I will bless You as long
as I live. Psalm 63:3-4 (TLB)

A new chapter in my life began in March, 2017. This new chapter is about a journey that God has been leading me through, a journey that began the morning when I heard, for the first time, the diagnosis that everyone dreads and hope they will never hear … … CANCER.

At times this journey has lead me through some deep valleys with dark and threatening shadows, finding myself in need of a courage and source of strength beyond my own to be able to press on. There were other times, when I have needed it most, that it has felt like I was being lifted up from the dark valley below by God's strong and loving arms to soar to the mountain top, where He blessed me by allowing me to see an incredibly majestic, glorious, and panoramic view of what ultimately lies ahead for those who remain faithful to Him.

Although there are many different forms of cancer - each comprised of its own unique set of symptoms, treatment plan and prognosis - that word "cancer" can often strike fear into the hearts and minds of even the strongest and bravest of people. Cancer is nondiscriminatory when it comes to things like wealth, position, power, status, education or ethnic background. No one is exempt from the possibility.

Often the immediate response from the patient, especially the first time they hear it, is unbelief, shock, fear, and uncertainty about their future. Their mind starts filling with questions like:

> How will this new diagnosis impact my life, my family, my goals and my plans?;
> How will the recommended treatments and related side effects affect my ability to do my job and continue to support my family?;
> How am I going to get through this?

So many questions. So few guarantees. The bigger questions on their minds and hearts, even when left unspoken, may be, "Will I die from this?", and "If I die, where will I go next?"

> Many Christians are familiar with the bible verse found in Romans 8:28 (NKJV),
> "And we know that all things work together for good to those who love God, to those who are the called according to His purpose."

Many Christians believe it's true, yet when they or a loved one is diagnosed with cancer they may begin to question, or even doubt, how this disease could possibly work for good. When their whole world, all they planned, seems to have been turned upside down, it's often hard to see it early on. That's when we need to accept by faith and trust that this promise is true, even though we don't yet see or understand how God will work this out for good. Though it may not be as clear in the beginning, if we remain faithful to Him it will probably be much easier to see the many ways that God actually **did** work it for good as we move further along in the journey.

Going through cancer in any form is never an easy experience.

Yet, as I look back over the past three years, I have seen and personally experienced that the promise of Romans 8:28 **is** true. Through it all, I can praise God for what He has taught me in the journey, what I have learned from The Master Teacher's hand. Life transforming, life enriching lessons about His faithfulness: to supply my needs in every situation; to comfort my anxious heart and give me peace in the storms of life; and to help me face and overcome the fear of death itself, by reminding me that the best is yet to come.

I can also praise Him for the many unexpected blessings in the journey: for the outpouring of love, prayers and support of family and friends; for providing hope, always when I have needed it the most and sometimes coming in very unexpected ways; and, most of all, for the timeless encouragement and comfort found in His Word, the bible.

In writing this book, I was especially encouraged and inspired by one of the most beloved and comforting passages in the bible, the 23rd Psalm that has blessed countless people through the ages:

> "The Lord is my shepherd; I shall not want.
> He makes me to lie down in green pastures; He leads me beside still waters.
> He restores my soul;
> He leads me in the paths of righteousness for His name's sake.
> Yea, though I walk through the valley of the shadow of death, I will fear no evil;
> For You are with me; Your rod and Your staff, they comfort me.
> You prepare a table before me in the presence of my enemies;
> You anoint my head with oil; my cup runs over.
> Surely goodness and mercy shall follow me all the days of my life;
> And I will dwell in the house of the Lord forever."
> Psalm 23 (NKJV)

God has taught me to appreciate and apply this very familiar psalm in some new ways that relate to my cancer. As a shepherd leads and guards his sheep, the Lord is my leader, provider and protector. When I allowed my life to get so busy that I failed to get the rest I needed, He loved me enough to take me firmly by the hand, made me to rest and be refreshed near beautiful green hillsides and beside peaceful waters, and restored my body and my spirit. Even when I walk through this valley called cancer, I will fear no evil for He is with me. I know that I can safely trust Him to lead me in paths of righteousness. When I follow Him, goodness and mercy shall follow me all my life. Best of all, when this mortal life is done I will be with Him forever.

If you are going though cancer, my prayer and hope in sharing my story with you are that you will discover and experience for yourself the comfort, courage, strength, hope, and peace that can be found in God and in His Word. I want to especially encourage you that you and I can indeed walk this journey, knowing that we do not have to walk it alone or in our own strength; because God is with us, and He has promised never to leave us nor forsake us.

For all of that and so much more …

We can praise God when we are on the mountain top,
and we can praise Him in the valley.

One

The Journey Begins

The Lord is my rock and my fortress and my deliverer;
the God of my strength, in whom I will
trust. —2 Samuel 22:2–3 (NKJV)

The week following my granddaughter Kirstin's wedding was busy as we prepared for her move to Wisconsin to start her married life with her husband, Adam. It was a very special week, a time of reflecting on so many special memories and experiences that she and I had shared over the years. By early evening, we were getting a little tired from our busy day of sorting and packing and paused for a few minutes to relax.

I am not sure what prompted me to place my hand on my neck as I relaxed. I've often wondered if it was God's hand guiding my hand, alerting me to a serious matter that needed my attention. When I rubbed the left side of my neck gently, I felt something I had never felt before: a lump. I decided to check it out further by feeling the right side of my neck to see if what I had felt was symmetrical but felt no lump there. Feeling the left side once again to be sure, it was unmistakable. There was a clearly definable, palpable, and even visible lump.

Even though there weren't any other signs or symptoms, I

knew that a lump on the neck could be serious and decided to have it checked out by my primary doctor, Mark Peterson, as soon as possible. When I called his office first thing the next morning, his receptionist said that he was in and was available to see me right away. After a careful examination, Dr. Peterson said, "I wish I had better news for you. I think you have lymphoma. We will need to run some tests to know for sure, but I have recently treated another patient with symptoms very similar to yours, and tests confirmed it was lymphoma." Sensing the impact of his tentative diagnosis, he compassionately added, "I hope I am wrong."

As I left his office and drove home, I tried to comprehend what I had just heard. "I wish I had better news for you. I think you have lymphoma … I hope I am wrong." I tried to rein in and steady my thoughts and fears by reminding myself that Dr. Peterson's diagnosis was only tentative until confirmed by tests.

My thoughts then transitioned to telling my family what Dr. Peterson had told me, and I tried to anticipate what their responses might be. When I arrived home, the first person with whom I shared the news was my son Wayne, who asked how things went at the doctor's office. I tried to answer his questions as calmly and objectively as possible, emphasizing nothing was for sure until confirmed. It didn't take long before the word spread among my other four adult children, and each one called to ask questions that were on their minds and to share their concerns. Since God had blessed me with exceptionally good health for well over seventy years, it must have been shocking to them to consider that their mom may now have a serious health problem. I tried to reassure them as much as I could while still trying to settle my own questions and fears.

The next three weeks were filled with medical appointments with an ENT doctor and oncologist, a variety of blood tests and scans, and finally a definitive biopsy. During this time, I tried to keep my focus on what I needed to do rather than on my feelings. It seemed like a very long three weeks.

Finally, by April 18, the results were all in, and each one confirmed Dr. Peterson's tentative diagnosis. The oncologist described it to my son Wayne, my daughter Laura, and me as a large, cancerous mass invading the neck, a smaller one next to it, and a small mass in the mediastinum. The official clinical name was stage 2 B Cell Non-Hodgkins Lymphoma, a form of cancer that starts in white blood cells called lymphocytes, which are part of the body's immune system.

Now that the definitive diagnosis was finally in, there could be no doubt. **I had cancer!**

I needed to steady my heart and my mind and confront that reality, but that would take time. I didn't know what the path ahead of me would be like. Even more importantly, I didn't know what the outcome would be at the other end of the journey.

What I did know, without a doubt, is that my confidence in this journey would need to be in the One who had walked with me throughout my life and sustained me during other times when I had gone through significant challenges. If my confidence were only in me to handle whatever lay ahead, I knew that I would probably fall short at times. But when my confidence is in my Heavenly Father, I know that He who has never failed me before will not fail me now and would be faithful to provide all that I might need in the future.

Two

Learning to Sing in My Heart

He has given me a new song to sing, of praises to our God.
Now many will hear of the glorious things he did for me, and
stand in awe before the Lord, and put their
trust in him. —Psalm 40:3 (TLB)

When I first met with Dr. Peterson about the lymphoma, there
were no signs or symptoms other than a lump on the side
of my neck. During the next few weeks, however, that began to
change in very significant ways. The tumor continued to grow until
it compromised the normal function of nearly every vital function
inside my neck.

One of the earliest signs of an escalating problem that I
experienced was feeling something inside my throat that prompted
me to try to cough it up. There were several mornings when I would
wake up from a sound sleep with very hard coughing spells that lasted
about fifteen minutes, hardly allowing me time to catch my breath.
One coughing spell was so severe that I briefly lost consciousness
and fell on the bathroom floor, waking up in severe pain from four
broken ribs and needing to be transported by ambulance to the
hospital.

The tumor began pressing against the esophagus, pushing part of it from its normal vertical form into a shelf-like, horizontal bar that made it impossible for me to swallow anything that wasn't in liquid form. It pressed against my vocal cords and totally took away my voice. Even more threatening, scans revealed that this tumor had encompassed the carotid artery and was pressing against the jugular vein.

After reviewing my medical records, my oncologist consulted with the radiation oncologist to develop a treatment plan. Even though the tumor was large, the radiation oncologist thought that it was localized enough to respond well to radiation therapy and seemed confident that it could ultimately be "resolved." He recommended daily radiation treatments be given Monday through Friday for a total of twenty treatments over the course of four weeks. The treatments began immediately while I was at the hospital and continued through most of May.

I tried to learn how to adapt to these recent changes and challenges during the weeks that followed. My first challenge was getting enough nutrition since I was only able to swallow liquids. My daughter-in-law, Carrie, was a real encouragement and blessing to me during these weeks, especially in meeting my nutritional needs. By using her exceptional knowledge of nutrition that she had cultivated over many years, she found so many ways to use her blender and juicer to create delicious smoothies and juices, often adding supplements such as whey to make them even better.

For nearly a month, I was unable to attend the Sunday morning worship services at my church, the Harvest New Beginnings Church in Oswego, Illinois. The first Sunday that I finally felt well enough to attend church, I eagerly looked forward to seeing my dear friends and sisters in Christ again, faithful "prayer warriors" who had been praying for me and had sent so many cards and notes of encouragement since I had become sick. I was deeply touched and blessed by the outpouring of their love that morning, when so many warmly welcomed me back with a hug and said, "I am praying for you."

One of my favorite parts of being in the worship services each Sunday had always been to join in the singing. Ever since I was a child, I had always loved to sing and could really get caught up in the beautiful melodies, lifting my voice with others in praise and worship to God. But when the congregation began to sing, I quickly realized that my inability to speak also made it impossible for me to join them in singing. The best that I could manage was to lip sync the words and sing silently in my heart. Ironically, the song that morning was "Oh for a Thousand Tongues to Sing". With a sad and disappointed heart, I prayed, "Oh Lord, I won't ask for a *thousand* tongues. Just please help this *one* tongue that You've given me to be able to sing Your praises again." What a blessing to know in times like these, our moments of deep disappointment, that we have a loving Heavenly Father who knows every thought that we think and every feeling in our hearts, sees every tear that we shed, hears our every prayer, and welcomes us to come to Him just as we are and be comforted. He heard my silent prayer that morning and assured me that, even though I had no voice, I could still sing to Him in my heart, and He would hear every silent word—loud and clear!

I am so thankful that a little further along in this journey God chose to bless me and restore my ability to speak again. My loss of speech was temporary, but for some it's permanent. Going through this time has helped me to better understand some of the challenges others experience who are permanently unable to speak. Even the ordinary pleasure of going to a favorite restaurant and sharing a meal with a friend becomes strained and awkward, when only one of you is able to speak and the conversation is one sided.

"I will sing to the Lord as long as I live. I
will praise God to my last breath!"
Psalm 104:33 (TLB)

Three

Called to Be God's Ambassador

How thankful I am to Christ Jesus our Lord for
choosing me as one of his messengers,
and giving me the strength to be faithful
to him. 1 Timothy 1:12 (TLB)

At first I noticed her from a little distance, as she entered the
waiting area of the Radiation / Oncology Department at the
Rush Copley Medical Center in Oswego, Illinois. Although I didn't
know Heather yet, she wore three things that day that revealed a lot
about her: a hospital gown; a turban, that I assumed was intended
to hide a side effect from her chemo treatments; and a radiant smile
that seemed to warm the small area we were both sitting in, as we
each waited to be called for treatment. I was feeling a little tired and
dispirited that day, but there was something about her radiant smile
that really encouraged and lifted up my heart.

During the next few weeks Heather and I became acquainted,
since our respective treatments were scheduled around the same time
each day Monday through Friday. My respect for her grew even more
when I learned that she was receiving **both** chemo and radiation
treatments to fight her cancer. Even though she was going through
her own health challenge, it was apparent that she was experiencing

a joy and peace that passes understanding from God. As time went on, she and I learned that we both loved the Lord and were "sisters in Christ", whose paths had briefly crossed by the divine plan of God.

The day finally came when she and I completed the last of our scheduled treatments. On "graduation day" the nurses greeted us with spirited congratulations and "high fives". During the weeks we were blessed to be together, Heather and I developed a special bond, travelers walking together through a valley to encourage each other for a season. We shed a few tears as we said our "goodbyes", shared a warm hug and sincerely wished each other well.

When I think of Heather and how much she encouraged me and lifted my spirit, I believe that God gave her an opportunity to use her journey with cancer for the purpose of encouraging other cancer patients she would meet at the hospital. Fighting the same disease, they could easily relate to her and be inspired by the courage, joy and peace that she demonstrated in the way she was dealing with her own cancer. It was as if she was appointed by God, to serve as His ambassador, to encourage those who were also walking though a difficult journey.

When our president commissions an ambassador to go to a foreign country, the ambassador must realize and always remember 1) that he represents someone greater than himself, and 2) his mission is to faithfully carry out the plan of the one who has chosen him. He may be sent to a friendly place, a nation whose values are similar to ours, to offer mutual support and to strengthen our respective countries' mutual alliance. At other times, he may be sent to a difficult place to serve, possibly to meet with a leader of a hostile nation in a war zone to negotiate a cease fire. In either case, whether it's to serve in a friendly or difficult place, the ambassador must be willing to go wherever he is sent. He must do his best to succeed in carrying out his appointed mission, knowing that his success or failure will ultimately reflect not only on him, but, even more important, will reflect on the one he represents.

I believe that God desires to use every Christian, everyone who has been saved and redeemed by the blood of Christ, to be an ambassador for Him. To be chosen as His ambassador, we need to be willing to go **wherever** He sends us, to carry out our assigned mission, and at all times remember that we represent The One who has commissioned us to go in His name. What we do, what we say, even our attitudes will not only reflect on who we are, but of even greater significance they will reflect, either for better or worse, on our God and Savior. By how we represent Him will either draw people to our Lord or turn them away.

> "How true it is that a servant is not greater than his master. Nor is the messenger more important than the one who sends him." John 13:16 (TLB)

> "And whatever you do or say, let it be as a representative of the Lord Jesus, and come with him into the presence of God the Father to give him your thanks." Colossians 3:17 (TLB)

As God's ambassadors, there are times that He may send us to a friendly place, an "ally," such as a group of like minded sisters and brothers in the family of God, to mutually encourage, edify, support, and pray for one another. Might be to serve in some capacity in our own local church or community. He may send us to visit, support, encourage, and befriend those who are too weak or ill to attend worship services as they had before.

But what if God's plan for you or for me, as His ambassador, is to be sent to a more difficult place to serve, like the Oncology Department at a hospital? What if our assigned mission required that we become one of the patients fighting cancer, for the purpose of offering encouragement and hope to the other patients we might meet in the hospital waiting room or the Infusion Lab. Would we be willing to accept His plan and go where He sends us, even when it's difficult? Is it reasonable or fair of God to ask us to make that kind of sacrifice? When I consider what Jesus sacrificed for us, the answer is clear. He left the glories of heaven and came to earth and was willing to sacrifice his life on the cross so that we could be saved. What sacrifice that God might ask of you or me could ever compare with that?

> "And so, dear brothers, I plead with you to give your bodies to God. Let them be a living sacrifice, holy - the kind he can accept. When you think of what he has done for you, is this too much to ask."
> Romans 12:1 (TLB)

Whatever the situation, wherever He chooses to send us, by allowing the Spirit of God to first work in us and then through us, we will be able to demonstrate how He can give the courage, hope, peace, and joy that goes beyond anything we could ever do on our own. Few things can encourage someone going through cancer more than a fellow cancer patient who is dealing with some of the same challenges, but with a joy and peace that passes understanding.

Sometimes all it takes is a willing heart and a smile!

Four

Thankful for the Blessings

Always be joyful. Always keep on praying.
No matter what happens,
always be thankful, for this is God's will for
you who belong to Christ Jesus.
I Thessalonians 5:16-18 (TLB)

The prescribed radiation treatments were completed by the end of May, 2017. Now it was just a matter of time to learn how effective the treatments were in "resolving" the tumor that had caused so many issues, including the loss of my voice and being unable to swallow anything other than liquids. Although I was eager to learn the result of radiation, the oncology radiologist cautioned me to allow up to four months following treatments for the radiation to continue to work. I would just have to wait patiently until summer's end, when a definitive PET scan would reveal how effective the radiation had been.

It wasn't easy to wait patiently, but there were some encouraging signs that things were beginning to get better. Little by little, week by week, I started to feel that my body was getting stronger. By mid-summer I was able to swallow soft foods again.

Gradually my voice began to return too. I first noticed it one

Sunday morning as I was driving to church. The car radio was tuned into WMBI, broadcasting the worship service from the Moody Memorial Church in Chicago. When the congregation began to sing, I started to lip sync to the music. To my surprise and delight, for the first time in weeks I heard a sound, **a real sound,** coming from my voice. A very quiet sound, to be sure. It was still more breath than notes, but I was actually singing again! I could hardly hold back the tears of joy. With each successive Sunday, my voice slowly grew stronger; and once again I was able to sing the beautiful praise and worship gospel songs and hymns.

Good parents usually teach their children at a very early age to say "Thank you" when they receive a gift. Likewise, God wants His children to appreciate and sincerely thank Him for all His wonderful blessings. Throughout my life there have been so many reasons to be thankful for God's loving kindness and His daily provision to meet my needs and the needs of my family. I sincerely thanked Him for the many times that He provided for my husband and me and our five children during their growing up years. I was even more thankful for God's sustaining grace and provision during some difficult seasons of life. He comforted and sustained me as a widow and helped me to find healing from grief and fullness of life again.

God has also used this journey with cancer to open my eyes and help me to appreciate and thank Him for other ordinary, everyday blessings like:

> The power of a stranger's friendly smile that lifted
> the spirit of another patient (me) in the waiting area
> of the hospital's Radiation/Oncology Department;
> For the ability to speak and to swallow;
> For the joy of being able to sing again;
> For the blessing of a restful night's sleep;
> And for so many other daily blessings that, up to
> now, I had taken for granted.

Throughout the summer of 2017 I thanked Him for the blessing of my family, especially for my daughter-in-law, Carrie, who was available and willing to help meet my nutritional needs until God restored my ability to swallow solid foods again. I thanked Him for the many expressions of love and prayers for healing, offered on my behalf from faithful "prayer warriors", and for God hearing and answering their prayers. The anxiously awaited PET scan was finally taken in early September, and the news was good. By the grace of God, the large tumor in my neck was totally resolved!

Finally I thank God for the greatest blessings of all:

> For the blessing of the profound freedoms we enjoy in this country, especially the freedom of religion;
> For the blessing of a truly God centered church;
> For the blessing of the love and fellowship of the family of God; and
> For the forgiveness of sins and for His undeserved gift of eternal life through the sacrifice of His only Son, Jesus.

Five

When God Has a Plan, He Also Prepares the Way

A man's heart plans his way, but the Lord directs his steps.
Proverbs 16:9 (NKJV)

I am convinced that the all wise, omniscient God, the One who created the world and continues to sustain it, who loves me with an everlasting love, is both infinitely far wiser than I am and worthy of my total confidence and trust in Him. So in those times when His plan for me is different than what I had planned - even when I don't understand it and **especially** when it is not easy - I need to trust Him and believe that His plan is best for me.

Encouraged by the result of the PET scan, that my tumor was "resolved", I began to make plans for this new season of life. My "master plan" was to sell my house, move into a beautiful retirement community and, after all was said and done, begin enjoying a simpler way of life. I prayed for God's guidance and began exploring several retirement communities and finally selected one that offered a ranch style duplex home, set on a beautiful and expansive campus. I proceeded to put my house on the market; and within 36 hours after it was listed, my realtor received two excellent offers. The final inspection and closing proceeded without a hitch. So far, everything was working according to what I had planned.

I was excited about moving into my new home; but as everyone who has ever moved knows, moving involves weeks of hard work and can be pretty exhausting. Even though I knew I was getting tired, I kept promising myself that there would be plenty of time to rest after the work was done. So after all the cartons were unpacked and I was finally settled, I began to relax and thank God for all He had provided: a lovely home, friendly neighbors, and even an opportunity to begin a Christian support group for widows on the campus.

Leisurely early evening strolls around the campus really refreshed my spirit, as I began to relax and take time to enjoy the rainbow of colors and fragrance of the flowers, the early spring buds beginning to blossom on the trees, the musical songs of the birds, the graceful beauty of the swans swimming in their ponds, and the faint rustle of leaves responding to a gentle breeze. The beauty of it all reminded me of a very familiar passage in Psalm 23:1-3 (NKJV)

> "The Lord is my shepherd, I shall not want. He makes me to lie down in green pastures; He leads me beside the still waters. He restores my soul."

At the next appointment with my oncologist in May, everything couldn't have gone better. My checkup was good and the blood tests were all within normal limits. When the doctor asked me how I was feeling, I could honestly respond that I was feeling very well. No symptoms or issues that I was aware of. All was good!

Even though everything was apparently great in May, just two months later things began to change. A moderate lower back pain in the mornings, a low grade fever and chills prompted me to call my primary doctor, Mark Peterson, who encouraged me to see my oncologist instead and promptly forwarded my information to him. The oncologist ordered several blood tests and wanted me to meet with him early the next morning to discuss his findings. With all these new and troubling symptoms, it was difficult not to worry about all the possibilities, all the "what ifs." My appointment with him the next morning only seemed to justify my fears and concerns. He explained that he was concerned about some troubling readings on the blood tests taken the day before and wanted me to schedule a PET scan and meet with him again as soon as possible afterward. I was both anxious to learn the result of the PET scan and yet concerned about what it might reveal, so I prayed that God would give me the courage to face the outcome, **whatever** that might be. A few days later I met with my oncologist again, and he indicated that the PET scan confirmed what he had suspected. The Non-Hodgkins Lymphoma had not only returned but had spread, metastasized throughout much of my body, including most of my spine, and was reclassified from a Stage II to a Stage IV.

His words brought a raw reality to my worst fears. I was in shock and struggled to comprehend what he was saying. How could this spread so far and so fast? Just ten months ago there was cause to celebrate. The cancerous tumor in my neck was totally "resolved." Even more puzzling were the two nearly perfect checkups since then, the first in February and the second in May, just two months before. My mind kept asking the same questions, "How can you feel so good, have several blood tests within the normal ranges, and even pass a physical exam - not once but twice?" "How could it spread that far undetected, without any signs or symptoms to alert either my doctor or me that a serious problem was developing silently, as if slipping under the radar?"

Although no one ever asks for pain or enjoys pain when it comes, I learned that there are times when a loving and compassionate God has a benevolent purpose for allowing the pain that we all experience in life from time to time. Pain often serves the purpose of getting our attention, alerting us that something is going on within us that is not normal and needs medical attention. The worse the pain, the sooner we respond. In my case, the absence of pain for several months allowed the cancer to grow undetected and was able to spread and advance from Stage II to Stage IV. God used the quickly escalating pain to get my attention and prompted me to seek medical attention and treatment. If it hadn't been for the pain, the cancer would have continued to grow undetected; and the outcome would undoubtedly have been much worse. Even though I didn't enjoy it - no one usually enjoys pain - as God planned, it worked for my good.

With each day the back pain steadily increased and became more disabling. The simple act of raising myself up from bed in the morning or laying myself down again at night were beyond what I could manage. The level 10 pain was just too severe. Within just a matter of a few weeks I had regressed from being fully independent to becoming completely dependent. It was clear that I would need somebody to be with me 24/7 to care for me. I am so grateful that my granddaughter, Rachel, and her husband, Matthew, were available and willing to stay with me for several months and help me until I was able to care for myself again.

No doubt about it, this sudden turn of events had definitely blindsided me; but it didn't take God unaware, for He knows what's in our future as well as the past. Although I cannot even begin to fully comprehend how the God who sustains the entire universe is also fully aware of what happens in the individual life of each of His children. Yet I know it's true. When our Heavenly Father with infinite wisdom and perfect love designs a specific plan for each of His children, He not only maps out the steps of the journey but also prepares the way before them. He may change our circumstances or move other people or ourselves into position, so that all those He has appointed will be ready to help us walk the journey He has planned.

When I reflected about all the changes that began in mid-summer of 2018, the return of my cancer and loss of independence for several months, I could see how God had prepared me and other people to help me walk the journey according to His perfect plan for my life and for theirs. He blessed the plan to sell my house in record time and moved me from a two story house into a home that was much smaller, a ranch style without stairs just three months before I became so disabled that using stairs would have been all but impossible. Eight months before I reached the point of needing someone to stay with me, Rachel and Matthew felt that God was directing them to move back into the area from South Carolina and were available to help and care for me when I needed their help. Seeing the hand of God work in so many ways for my good increased my confidence that I could safely place myself in His hands now and trust my future to Him.

> "Trust in the Lord with all your heart, and
> lean not on your own understanding;
> in all your ways acknowledge Him, and He shall
> direct your paths." Proverbs 3:5-6 (NKJV)

Six

A Shower of Blessings

In response to all he has done for us, let us
outdo each other in being helpful
and kind to each other and in doing good. Hebrews 10:24 (TLB)

I n the days leading up to the first chemotherapy treatment, I tried
to prepare myself for what might lie ahead. I wondered about
whether I might experience some of the more common side effects
of chemo drugs like hair loss, severe nausea or fatigue.

It really helped to put some of these fears to rest when the
oncology nurse encouraged me to meet with her for an individual
class about chemotherapy prior to my first treatment. She used
that opportunity to help prepare me by explaining what I might
expect from the treatments and then patiently and compassionately
answered all my questions. She explained that since my cancer
was progressing slowly, the oncologist had decided to manage it
in a palliative, less aggressive manner. The goal in my case was not
about aiming for a total remission or cure, but treating it more like
a chronic health condition with periodic episodes that would be
treated as they occurred. This palliative treatment plan would use
milder chemotherapy drugs that would produce fewer side effects
and would be easier for me to tolerate.

I prayed that God would calm my anxious heart and give me His peace as my daughter, Laura and I headed to the Oncology Clinic for the first chemotherapy treatment. As it turned out, there were several things that blessed me and helped the day go much better than I had expected. The oncology nurse greeted us and lead Laura and me to the open and spacious infusion room surrounded by individual cubicles. Each cubicle was furnished with a comfortable, adjustable recliner chair for the patient, another chair for a guest, and a television set. She calmly explained each step of the process, regularly stopping to ask if I had any questions. After connecting the IV tubing to my surgically implanted port, she did everything she could to help me feel as comfortable as possible during my treatment: "Would you like a heated blanket?", "May I get you some small packages of cookies and crackers or a bottle of water or juice?", Feel free to move around the room, and just let me know if there is anything more that I can do for you. I will be right here if you need anything."

In the days prior to this, news about my second round with cancer was quickly shared with my family, friends and many of their friends on Facebook, friends in my Prime Timers Sunday School Class, and at Wednesday evening prayer meetings at my church. Cards began to fill up my mailbox nearly every day, but Laura encouraged me to wait to open them until the first day of chemotherapy treatment. Now that the awaited day had come, the big stack of cards waiting to be opened was like a wonderful Card Shower of Blessings. What a joy, what comfort, and what an encouragement as Laura and I opened each card. Each one unique with its own beautiful picture and verse, but all conveying the same loving message, "*Thinking of you and praying for you.*" I was truly humbled and very grateful for all the love expressed in those cards. They comforted and reassured me that I was not going through this challenging time alone. The prayers of many faithful "prayer warriors" were being lifted up to our Heavenly Father on my behalf. My heart was deeply touched by the love and prayers of so many, that tears just seemed to come easily.

After all the cards were opened, Laura and I began to explore the larger infusion area outside our cubicle. I had been assured that I was free to move around the room, as long I took my "best friend Ivy", my IV pole, with me. As I glanced around the room, I was impressed by how attractive it was; light and airy, with an entire wall of windows that looked out onto a lovely courtyard garden with flowers, trees and a fountain. The room was simply furnished with several desks for the nurses, some recliner chairs for patients receiving a shorter infusion, comfortable chairs for watching TV, and a couple of card tables, one with a jigsaw puzzle in progress tempting anyone who was interested in finding the next piece.

It didn't take more than a minute or two for Laura and me to "stake out our claim" for the day, one of the card tables. We both love to play games, so we came fully prepared and equipped with a few of our favorite card and dice games. Games like *Yahtze* or *Fill or Bust*, small enough for them all to fit inside a quart sized plastic storage bag and would only need a small space to play. We soon got so caught up in the usual spirit of friendly (and at times a little noisy) competition that the nurse had to come over to see what all the laughter and excitement were about. As my very wise daughter had planned, the games we played served a dual purpose. They provided a fun way to pass the time and also served as a welcome distraction from the chemo drugs that were very slowly dripping through my IV tube into my body for five+ hours.

This chemotherapy infusion was the first of six monthly cycles, each cycle consisting of coming to the clinic for three consecutive days: the first day for blood tests and to meet with the doctor; the second long 5+ hour day for the infusion; and a third day for another shorter infusion. I was so grateful and blessed that Laura was available and willing to take time off from her job to join me on the long infusion day for each of the six months.

Although the infusions were painless, the medications I received to offset potential side effects actually produced some side effects of their own. The main side effect I experienced was insomnia, that caused me to feel very tired, yet unable to sleep for several nights. I was blessed and thankful for a team of volunteers from my church, who brought several complete dinners the first week of every month, the week of chemotherapy, when I experienced the most fatigue. Other friends called or came to encourage and pray with me. As God often does, He used each visit to bring a mutual blessing. I was blessed by their kindness, their visits and meals; and they were blessed as I shared with them the ways that God was faithfully supplying all that I needed each day in this journey through the valley. The mutual blessings for believers who serve and encourage one another in the Lord was expressed in Romans 1:11-12 (TLB)

"For I long to visit you, so that I can impart to you the faith
that will help your church grow strong in the
Lord. Then, too, I need your help,
for I want not only to share my faith with
you but to be encouraged by yours:
Each of us will be a blessing to the other."

Seven

Facing the "Giants" - Fear and Discouragement

Fear not, for I am with you; be not dismayed, for I am your God.
I will strengthen you, yes, I will help you, I will
uphold you with My righteous right hand.
Isaiah 41:10 (NKJV)

Whenever we go through a prolonged period of illness that's often accompanied by pain, weakness or even exhaustion, we can become more vulnerable to the "giants" of fear and discouragement. Those times when we are tested to the limit of our endurance, fear and discouragement can appear like formidable giants lurking just outside the door of our mind and spirit, waiting for us to open that door and allow them to come in.

Even as Christians, when we are physically or emotionally spent, struggling to face another day of ongoing pain, tests, or procedures, it gets progressively easier for us to open that door. If and when that happens, we can be encouraged that we are not alone. Some of the strongest heroes of the faith, those who accomplished great successes for the Lord in the face of overwhelming odds against them, also suffered through times of fear, discouragement and even depression.

Elijah was one of the greatest prophets in the Old Testament. His most memorable victory for God was his literal mountaintop experience on Mount Carmel, where he stood alone and challenged the 450 false prophets of Baal and successfully defeated them. In spite of this incredible feat, when Queen Jezebel vowed to take revenge and kill him the very next day, Elijah had to flee for his life into the wilderness. He was so physically exhausted and spiritually discouraged that,

> "He prayed that he might die, and said, 'It is enough! Now, Lord, take my life, for I am no better than my fathers!'" I Kings 19:4 (NKJV)

David, another hero of the faith, was described in Acts 13:22 (NKJV) as a "man after (God's) own heart". Anointed by the prophet Samuel in his teens and filled with the Spirit of God, David was so courageous that he volunteered to represent the entire nation of Israel in defending itself against the giant Goliath, the man chosen to represent the Philistine army, an entire army of giants, in a one on one battle, winner take all. The odds appeared to be stacked against David. Compared to Goliath, David was too small, too young and too inexperienced in warfare to be the likely victor. Yet, in spite of these overwhelming odds, David overcame the giant Goliath with a single stone and a slingshot. In one day, David was catapulted from being a common shepherd to become a national hero and Israel's next king.

Not long after this incredible victory David spent years as a fugitive, fleeing into the desert from King Saul who was intent on killing him. During these extremely difficult and exhausting years, there were times when he also felt overwhelmed and desperate, as he expressed so honestly in Psalm 142:1-3 (TLB).

> "How I plead with God, how I implore His mercy, pouring out my troubles before Him. For I am

24

overwhelmed and desperate, and you alone know which way I ought to turn to miss the traps my enemies have set for me."

What helped David, that amazing warrior and defender of Israel, when he was fearful and, at times, even desperate? David remembered to look upward to find the strength and courage he desperately needed,

> "Then I prayed to Jehovah, 'Lord,' I pled, 'you are my only place of refuge. Only you can keep me safe. Hear my cry, for I am very low. Rescue me from my persecutors, for they are too strong for me." Psalm 142: 5-6 (TLB)

> "Yea, though I walk through the valley of the shadow of death, I will fear no evil; for You are with me; Your rod and Your staff, they comfort me." Psalm 23:4 (NKJV)

> "My eyes are upon You, O God the Lord; in You I take refuge." Psalm 141:8 (NKJV)

David's inspiring words of faith and confidence in God during those times when he "walked through the valley" can encourage us. We are fully engaged in a different kind of battle, possibly the biggest battle of our lifetime, against a formidable foe called cancer. We're not fighting against a giant of a man like Goliath, but rather an enemy made up of rogue cells and molecules, so minuscule in size that they are visible only to the trained eye of a doctor who surveys our enemy through a microscope. In the process of fighting this enemy, there probably will be days when we experience battle fatigue. Times when "the giants" of fear and discouragement threaten to overcome us and rob our very soul of the peace of God.

Like David we can find the strength and courage we need to face our "giants" by remembering to look upward and come humbly before our God in prayer. We need to openly and honestly tell Him about the struggle we are going through, that we desperately need His help in the battle we are engaged. When we feel especially low, we can ask Him for a very strong sense of the presence of His Holy Spirit surrounding us, like a divine and impenetrable wrap of armor, to protect us from the enemy, whatever giant that threatens us. We can admit that the battle is bigger than we are, but deeply thankful that He is bigger still. We can find comfort in knowing that the omniscient God fully knows our every need, yet He still wants us to come and acknowledge that we need Him. When our plans are shattered, our courage fails, our physical strength is spent, and our hearts are heavy, we can be assured that our Heavenly Father will warmly welcome us, as a loving father welcomes and comforts his hurting child. He will neither judge us nor scold us for being weak or heart broken, but will instead embrace and comfort us with His love. Whatever breaks your heart or mine touches the very heart of God.

We can also find great comfort, encouragement and peace in regularly reading and meditating on The Word of God, the bible, in passages like:

"The Lord is near to those who have a broken heart, and saves such as have a contrite spirit." Psalm 34:18 (NKJV)

"God is our refuge and strength, a very present help in trouble. Therefore we will not fear, even though the earth be removed, and though the mountains be carried into the midst of the sea." Psalm 46:1-2 (NKJV)

"I will lift up my eyes to the hills - from whence comes my help? My help comes from the Lord, who made heaven and earth." Psalm 121:1-2 (NKJV)

"Don't worry about anything; instead, pray about everything; tell God your needs, and don't forget to thank him for his answers. If you do this, you will experience God's peace, which is far more wonderful than any human mind can understand. His peace will keep your thoughts and your hearts quiet and at rest as you trust in Christ Jesus." Philippians 4:6-7 (TLB)

If God could help David conquer the giants, won't He also help you and me to overcome the giants in our lives. He is greater than our greatest fear. We can either be overcome by fear and discouragement, or we can overcome them by the power of the Holy Spirit. He Who dwells within us is able to give us the courage we need, take away our fears, calm our troubled spirit, and give us His peace that passes understanding.

"Yet in all these things we are more than conquerors through Him who loved us." Romans 8:37 (NKJV)

Eight

Finding Hope When You Need It

Now may the God of hope fill you with
all joy and peace in believing,
that you may abound in hope by the power of the Holy Spirit.
Romans 15:13 (NKJV)

A few months after my series of six monthly cycles of chemo treatments finally came to an end, I was more than ready for a refreshing change of scenery. So when the opportunity came to spend a week with my 17 year old granddaughter, Whitney, at the beautiful Gull Lake Ministries Center, in Hickory Corners, Michigan, I was eager to go. It's a wonderful place where a Christian family can go to experience wholesome family fun and fellowship.

One beautiful sunny afternoon that week I planned to take a walk down to the lake and quietly reflect on the beauty of it all. For a few hours I decided to redirect my thoughts above my health challenges and refresh my spirit by lifting up my eyes toward the heavens and remember that God is still there. As I often do, I prayed before I started my trek that God would guide me to a few people that He wanted me to interact with. Maybe someone like myself who needed a word of encouragement or a little hope for whatever they might be struggling with. Whenever I allow God to direct my steps in this way, it's something like a spiritual adventure. I never know in advance who that person might be; but when He directs me to them, it always turns out to be a mutual blessing. So I leisurely strolled along the beach, taking some time to briefly visit with a few women I met along the way.

Eventually my stroll took me farther down past the beach to an area designated for family fun in deeper water. I noticed another woman standing nearby who was watching her husband and children as they climbed aboard the "rocket boat," a family favorite six passenger inflatable ride pulled by a speedboat for a fun filled, fun soaked "adventure at sea". We had barely begun to get acquainted, when she asked me, "Have you had cancer?"

Her question took me by surprise. "I have, but how did you know?"

"I noticed that your water bottle was from "Phil's Friends" (a Christian ministry founded by Phil Zielka, a two time cancer survivor, that seeks to encourage patients going through cancer). Then she continued, "I am familiar with that ministry. I am an oncology nurse and work in an infusion lab, where I administer chemo drugs to patients when they come in for their treatment*s.*"

As we continued to get better acquainted, I began to share with her about a book that I was in the process of writing about my journey with cancer that I hoped the Lord would use to encourage other cancer patients and give them hope.

She abruptly excused herself and promised, "I will be right back. There's something I want to give to you." She definitely had my curiosity peaked. A few minutes later she hurried back and said, "My family and I were out walking this morning and found this stone on the beach. I'd like to give it to you." She handed me the small stone, not much longer than an inch or so, indistinguishable in every way from all the other small stones on the beach, except for one thing. Written on one side was a message, a one word message that somebody had apparently written on it before tossing it into the lake, possibly praying that it would be discovered by someone who needed an encouraging word. The one word message was Hope", and it was God's gift that morning to someone who really needed a fresh filling of hope ... ... me.

HOPE! When your world as you knew it is turned upside down. When the plans you've made are interrupted or even upended, we need hope. Some have even said that we can live about forty days without food, three or four days without water, but we can't live a day without hope.

HOPE! Prisoners of war, held captive for months or even years under the most deplorable and insufferable conditions, were asked upon their eventual rescue and release, "How did you manage to survive, when some of the other prisoners didn't?" Their simple answer, "I never gave up hope that some day I would be rescued." Hope, especially when their situation seemed hopeless, gave them the inner strength and the will to persevere another day and helped to keep them alive until they were rescued..

When we are dealing with the ongoing challenges and demands of battling our way through a serious illness like cancer, hope is an absolute necessity if we are to keep fighting on. Hope will motivate us to be willing to take another test, go through another procedure, and can give us the will to survive another day, rather than surrender to the enemy that ceaselessly and relentlessly is attacking our body.

HOPE! A small word, but I am convinced that it is as essential and indispensable to a healthy life - encompassing our emotional, physical, mental, and spiritual health - as the food we eat, the air we breathe, and even a shelter to protect us from the elements. It may be possible to function without hope; but to really push through the difficult times in life, we need hope.

So where can we go, who can we turn to, to find that very essential hope to help and sustain us during difficult times? Without a doubt, there is no one better that we can turn to in our hour of need than the Lord. The One who loves us, knows our every thought and feeling, sees our every struggle, and invites us to come to Him just as we are and is totally able to meet our needs.

I remember one particular morning when I was especially discouraged and feeling like I needed a serious emergency "infusion" of hope to get through some difficult days. So during my morning devotional hour, I came to the throne of Heaven and prayed, "Oh, Lord, I am struggling this morning. I really need hope in this journey I am walking through. First I want to thank you, Lord, for the confident hope that when this life is done I will be with You in a far better place. But until that appointed time comes, I need a confident hope for each day that will assure me that I can get through whatever the day brings and be able to keep on going."

With perfect compassion and love, He answered, "The confident hope you need for each day is that I will be with you and will provide whatever you need for that day."

Once again, my loving Heavenly Father supplied exactly what I needed. A confident hope, not just for that day but for every day that followed. He reminded me that no matter what might happen, I could depend on Him to supply **whatever** I might need to get through each day. His answer to my prayer reminded me of what Jesus said in His Sermon on the Mount,

> "So don't be anxious about tomorrow. God will take
> care of your tomorrow too. Live one day at a time."
> Matthew 6:34 (TLB)

That precious gift with its message, "Hope", given to me by a stranger as God directed our paths to cross while we sat by the lake one early summer day, is sitting on my computer desk where I regularly see it. It serves as a daily reminder on Whom my confident hope for that day **must** rest. I was often encouraged in the challenging months that lay ahead of me that God is, and must continue to be, my ultimate hope in this journey through cancer.

Nine

From Giving Help to Needing Help

When God's children are in need,
you be the one to help them out. Romans 12:13 (TLB)

For most of my adult life, I have been the one taking care of others, trying to do my best to help meet their needs. As a mother of five, I was very busy taking care of my children's needs when they were growing up. When my husband went through many years of poor health, I tried to meet his needs until God called him home. Seventeen months later, my 87 year old mother-in-law, Dallas, came to live with my daughter, Laura, and me after she lost her only other child, her daughter Marion, who had been her caregiver. I was my mother's closest companion and helper after she became a widow and, by God's grace and providence, was at her bedside when she went home to be with the Lord.

After my oldest son, Jeff, who had suffered through a serious medical challenge and lengthy recovery, was finally well enough to attend church again, I would drive nearly an hour and a half round trip to bring him to church on Sunday mornings and drive him back again in the afternoon. I just thanked God for sparing his life and that he was finally well enough to be able to attend church again. When a friend at church commented on how nice it was for me to pick him up, I simply responded without hesitating, "When I considered whether I would rather be the one giving the help or be the one needing help, I would much rather be the one giving the help." Little did I know when I said, "I would rather be the one giving the help", that within just a few weeks cancer would dramatically change my life again, including my ability to help others. My role would reverse from the one who gives help to become the one who needed others to help me.

For the first time in my life, I would soon learn from personal experience about some of the special challenges we face when we become the ones who need help. God used this new and unfamiliar experience to help me learn several very important life lessons, lessons that have enriched my life by helping me to grow in empathy and compassion. Through what I've learned, I am better prepared to understand and minister to others in need as He gives me opportunity and ability.

One of the first things I've learned, when cancer strikes and you are the one in need of help, is that it can be very humbling. Whether I was caring for others or trying to meet my own needs, I was typically very reluctant to ask for help. Even when help was offered, I would usually decline, "Thanks for your offer, but I'm OK. I can do it." That perspective may be commendable in some ways and make us very responsible people, but it can also nurture within us a spirit of independence and pride. We can unintentionally become the super hero of our own narrative. It takes courage and a humble heart to prayerfully ask God, as David did, to regularly search our hearts and see if our attitude and motivation behind even our good works is pleasing and acceptable to Him.

"Search me, O God, and know my heart; try me, and know my thoughts; and see if there be any wicked way in me, and lead me in the way everlasting." Psalm 139:23-24 (KJV)

Another thing I've learned in this journey is that we all need help at times. It can be one way that God uses some difficult times in life to remind us that we not only need others but, even more important, we need Him. So if we all experience times when the challenges we face are beyond what we can do, we need to be honest with ourselves and admit that we need help. To be willing to accept sincere offers of help or, to go a step further, even solicit the help of others according to our needs.

Many people who experience serious health issues, that due to declining strength and abilities become increasingly dependent on family members for some level of care, will think or say, "I don't want to be a burden to my family." Even when a family member willingly offers help or goes further and invites their loved one to move into their home to care for them, the thought of becoming a burden to their family leaves them with a very heavy feeling of sadness and guilt. They may also be reluctant to burden their friends by asking them for help.

It really helps to resolve that feeling of guilt and give us peace, when we remember that God has already provided a gracious and loving plan for His children. He desires and directs us to mutually love and serve one another, especially in time of need. God's plan applies to our earthly family, as well as our family in Christ.

> "But if anyone does not provide for his own, and especially for those of his household, he has denied the faith and is worse than an unbeliever." 1 Timothy 5:8 (NKJV)

"A friend loves at all times, and a brother is born for adversity." Proverbs 17:17 (NKJV)

Jesus even considers our love and service for one another the same as if we did it for Him. Jesus said in Matthew 25:34-40 (NKJV):

> "Then the King will say to those on His right hand, 'Come, you blessed of My Father, inherit the kingdom prepared for you from the foundation of the world: for I was hungry and you gave Me food; I was thirsty and you gave Me drink; I was a stranger and you took Me in; I was naked and you clothed Me; I was sick and you visited Me; I was in prison and you came to Me.' Then the righteous will answer Him, saying, 'Lord, when did we see You hungry and feed You, or thirsty and give You drink? When did we see You a stranger and take You in, or naked and clothe You? Or when did we see You sick, or in prison, and come to You?' And the King will answer and say to them, 'Assuredly, I say to you, inasmuch as you did it to one of the least of these My brethren, you did it to Me.'"

When we consider God's plan, that we love and care for one another, it frees us from feelings of guilt to being grateful. From a heart of gratitude, we can then sincerely thank God for how He has provided, once again, by moving the hearts of those around us to help us in our time of need. Recognizing that this is God's plan and provision for us, we then need to also sincerely express our gratitude to our family and/or others and let them know how much we appreciate their sacrificial acts of service and love

One practical and essential way to engage the help of others is to develop a personal support team. Family and friends may want to help us but aren't sure of exactly what kind of help we need. So we can help others to help us by communicating specifically how we'd like them to help. Do you need someone to help you with transportation to medical appointments? It can be also be very helpful to have a family member or trusted friend accompany you to medical appointments, who will be a second "set of ears" to listen to the doctor's comments and take notes about what was said. Would you enjoy having someone keep you company during long chemo treatments? A spirited competitive hour or two playing games or engaging in a hobby like scrapbooking can be a very pleasant and helpful means of distracting your attention from the slow and steady drip of the infusion drugs. Your church family or other friends can help provide meals on long and tiring chemo days. Do you need help with household chores or picking up some groceries? Do you need some financial assistance to help pay for medical expenses? On days when you feel down or discouraged, you may be encouraged by having a close friend or loved one simply sit beside you and quietly listen, while you honestly share what's on your heart and mind. A good friend will love you and want to support you with their time, touch, talk and tears and, most important of all, will commit to continually pray with you and for you.

> So you can help others to help you by:
> Defining what kind of help you need and/or would enjoy,
> Sharing your needs with others,
> Accepting offers of help with a grateful heart,
> Telling those who help you how much you appreciate what they do, and
> Praising God for His faithfulness and provision for your needs.

Finally if God's plan is to heal your body and renew your strength, you may have the opportunity to "pay it forward" by blessing others in need as you have been blessed.

Ten

Persevere with a Purpose

Rejoicing in hope, patient in tribulation,
continuing steadfast in prayer.
Romans 12:12 (NKJV)

There are times when we are fighting against a challenging disease, like cancer in its various forms, that it's hard to keep on going. When the battle seems more like a marathon than a sprint. When our spirit is willing, but our bodies are weak. When we just long for the pain of the journey to be over, so we can get back to life as we knew it before cancer struck.

So what can help us persevere in the face of hardship? It's comforting to learn that our all knowing, omniscient and loving Heavenly Father knows exactly what we are going through. Not a thing happens in our lives that He is unaware of or that takes Him by surprise. He knows our struggles, hears our sighs, and sees every tear that we shed. It helps to learn and remember when we are going through a season of suffering that a loving God has a good plan and purpose for whatever we may be experiencing, including cancer. His purpose for allowing us to experience hardship and suffering is intended to work for good, **especially** in the lives of His children.

"We know that all things work together for good to them that love God, to them who are the called according to his purpose." Romans 8:28 (KJV)

When we're hurting and needy, even when we don't understand how it could possibly work for good, these are the times when it's even more important that we need to walk through this valley by faith and not by sight. Some may doubt God's goodness when going through the storms of life. When they don't clearly see His purpose in the storm, they prefer to live by *seeing is believing,* refusing to believe until they can see. Rather than refusing to believe until we see God's purpose, it's essential for us to exercise faith in God and live by *believing is seeing.* Even though we don't always understand it at the time, that's when it's most important to believe the assurance we're given in His Holy Word and totally trust that it is true. God may in time open our "spiritual eyes" and give us new vision, helping us to see it all more clearly through His eyes.

"Now faith is the substance of things hoped for, the evidence of things not seen." Hebrews 11:1 (KJV)

One of God's purposes in allowing His children to experience trials is intended, by divine design, **to build up our faith and mature us as believers:**

"We also glory in tribulations, knowing that tribulation produces perseverance; and perseverance, character; and character, hope." Romans 5:3-4 (NKJV)

"Dear brothers, is your life full of difficulties and temptations? Then be happy, for when the way is rough, your patience has a chance to grow. So let it grow, and don't try to squirm out of your problems.

For when your patience is finally in full bloom, then you will be ready for anything, strong in character, full and complete." James 1:2-4 (TLB)

God also uses trials **to test our faith:**
"So be truly glad! There is wonderful joy ahead, even though the going is rough for a while down here. These trials are only to test your faith, to see whether or not it is strong and pure. It is being tested as fire tests gold and purifies it - and your faith is far more precious to God than mere gold; so if your faith remains strong after being tried in the test tube of fiery trials, it will bring you much praise and glory and honor on the day of His return." 1 Peter 1:6-7 (TLB)

In our weakness, **we discover God's strength:**
"They that wait upon the Lord shall renew their strength; they shall mount up with wings as eagles; they shall run, and not be weary; and they shall walk, and not faint." Isaiah 40:31 (KJV)

"The Lord is my rock and my fortress and my deliverer; my God, my strength, in whom I will trust; my shield and the horn of my salvation, my stronghold." Psalm 18:2 (NKJV)

"I can do all things through Christ who strengthens me." Philippians 4:13 (NKJV)

"We are praying, too, that you will be filled with his mighty, glorious strength so that you can keep on going no matter what happens - always full of the joy of the Lord." Colossians 1:11 (TLB)

Our trials are designed by God **to help us grow in understanding, empathy, and compassion for others**. It's nearly impossible for anyone to fully understand what someone else is going through, until they have first walked through a similar journey themselves. Once we've experienced cancer ourselves, we are better prepared to understand and encourage others who are going through cancer:

> "What a wonderful God we have - he is the Father of our Lord Jesus Christ, the source of every mercy, and the one who so wonderfully comforts and strengthens us in our hardships and trials. And why does he do this? So that when others are troubled, needing our sympathy and encouragement, we can pass on to them this same help and comfort God has given us." 2 Corinthians 1:3-4 (TLB)

Finally, it's very important for you and me to remember that our lives are more than just about us. What we say and do, how we respond to whatever trials God allows us to experience can, and often will, impact the lives of others, especially those who choose to follow our example. So we need to strive, with the strength and power of the Holy Spirit that dwells within the heart and soul of each believer, to persevere through difficult times in a way that will encourage others to draw nearer to God and find He is able to sustain them.

> "So take a new grip with your tired hands, stand firm on your shaky legs, and mark out a straight, smooth path for your feet so that those who follow you, though weak and lame, will not fall and hurt themselves but become strong." Hebrews 12:12-13 (TLB)

Eleven

Make Time for Some R&R

He makes me to lie down in green pastures;
He leads me beside the still waters.
He restores my soul. Psalm 23:2-3 (NKJV)

As we get older - or to be kinder, more mature and wiser because of what we have learned from life experience - we need to be more intentional about implementing good health habits. Even though we aren't able to control all the things that can affect our health, we **are** responsible for both knowing and incorporating into our lifestyle the things that have been proven to promote good health. Guided by medical professionals who can help us develop and implement: 1) an appropriate exercise plan; 2) an eating plan based on our metabolism, level of activity, and medical issues; and 3) an awareness and vigilance to be watchful for early warning signs of impending serious health conditions or disease.

In addition to the above, I've learned that it's very important for our mental, emotional, and spiritual health to develop a well balanced lifestyle made possible by asking God for wisdom and guidance regarding setting priorities that will help us balance the time and energy we spend on:

Work with rest,
Responsibility with recreation, and
Time we give to others with some quiet time spent alone with God

I am hard wired to enjoy setting goals and then working hard to accomplish them. My mother described anyone having these character traits as being "a doer", a high praise in her opinion. She instilled within me at an early age a good work ethic by assigning me a list of age appropriate chores and responsibilities, along with her promise, "When your chores are done, you may go out to play." It definitely motivated and worked for me as a child, but in my adult years there always seems to be something more that needs to be done.

At the start of a new year, I usually take time to make up my list of what I hope to accomplish in the year ahead. On Monday mornings I plan my goals for the week, and every morning I consult my goals for the week and from it make up my "To Do" list for the day. It's been helpful in giving me a sense of purpose, direction and accomplishment. Unfortunately, it's also had a serious downside. In trying so hard to accomplish some kind of apparently necessary work or responsibility, too often I have sacrificed the need to balance the time spent on work or responsibility with sufficient time to rest. My good intention to take time to rest as soon as the work was done was often preempted and disregarded by "the tyranny of the urgent".

If you are like me, there are times when we are just plain slow learners. Slow to identify and learn from some poor decisions and choices that we make in life. Unfortunately, until we learn from our mistakes, we are destined to repeat them and suffer the related consequences. It was only after my third episode with lymphoma within three years that I finally recognized a common thread, a pattern that very likely weakened my immune system and ultimately was a contributing factor to reactivate my lymphoma. Each episode was preceded by several months of unusually high activity: planning a family wedding; selling a house, packing up and moving into a new home; and a major responsibility that took the entire summer to complete. In my desire to meet each challenge, I disregarded my need to balance the extra activity and related stress with the need for additional rest. Although I was well aware each time that I was pushing myself too hard for too long, I kept promising myself that there would be time to rest after the work was done. Although I didn't see it for over two years, the correlation between prolonged periods of increased activity and decreased health, it finally became clearer to me while I was recovering from my third episode. It wasn't really too hard to connect the dots. Forced by pain and limited physical mobility, I had to set aside my usual busy schedule and finally made time to rest.

Our Creator, the One who formed us and without a doubt knows what we need better than we do, has set wise guiding principles intended to help us live healthier lives. I have learned to have a fresh appreciation for God's wisdom and love for His children expressed in His commandment regarding the need to balance work with rest. Though it was given to Moses thousands of years ago on two tablets of stone, it is still an essential principle for us to live by today.

> "Six days you shall labor and do all your work, but the seventh day is the Sabbath of the Lord your God. In it you shall do no work." "For in six days the Lord made the heavens and the earth, the sea and all that is in them, and rested the seventh day."
> Exodus 20:9-10a,11 (NKJV)

Although the New Testament church began gathering to worship on the first day of the week instead of the seventh, as a way to celebrate and honor Christ's resurrection, the principle of setting aside one day a week for rest and worship is still wise. Jesus encouraged His disciples to take time to rest after they returned from a very busy and successful day of ministry.

"Then Jesus suggested, 'Let's get away from the crowds for a while and rest.' For so many people were coming and going that they scarcely had time to eat." Mark 6:31 (TLB)

After sharing the gospel and ministering to the ever present crowds that often followed Him wherever He went, Jesus performed the miracle of feeding 5,000 men plus women and children with just five loaves of bread and two fish. By the end of that amazing day, Jesus also grew tired and felt the need to get away from the crowds and His disciples to rest and be alone with His Heavenly Father to pray.

"When He had sent the multitudes away, he went up into a mountain apart to pray; and when the evening was come, he was there alone." Matthew 14:23 (KJV)

I am so thankful that God is so wise, so loving and merciful. When I failed to take time out to rest, He used my cancer to set me apart from my busyness for awhile and rest. When I did, He strengthened my body and restored my soul.

Twelve

When Healing Isn't Promised

Blessed be the Lord, because He has heard
the voice of my supplications!
The Lord is my strength and my shield; my
heart trusted in Him, and I am helped;
therefore my heart greatly rejoices, and
with my song I will praise Him.
Psalm 28:6-7 (NKJV)

Encouraged by a good report from my oncologist, that the chemotherapy I had received from September, 2018 through February, 2019 had been successful in dealing with my second flareup with cancer, I was looking forward to resuming a more normal life again. But by mid- October, 2019, things quickly changed when a pain in my right leg rapidly progressed to a level #10 in a matter of just a few weeks. Every step I took brought severe pain, sending me to the hospital for five days. New scans and multiple tests confirmed the tentative diagnosis: a new tumor encroaching into a lumbar vertebrae was pressing against the sciatic nerve. Prescribed treatment: ten radiation treatments to shrink the tumor and relieve the extreme pain I was experiencing.

That very disappointing diagnosis, my third episode with

Non-Hodgkins Lymphoma within less than three years, forced me to face an uncomfortable reality. A reality that, up to now I either hadn't fully grasped or perhaps wasn't willing to face ... apart from a miracle my cancer would **never** be "**cured**". It wasn't really new information. It wasn't like I hadn't been told that before. I remembered that the nurse in the infusion lab, prior to my first chemotherapy the year before, had tried to describe and compassionately prepare me for the journey ahead. She encouraged me to think of my cancer as a chronic disease, treatable but not curable. She explained that because of my age and the slow progression of my specific form of Non-Hodgkins Lymphoma, it would be treated in a less aggressive, more tolerable, palliative manner with fewer side effects. "It's like a game of Whack-a-Mole. Whenever a mass develops enough to produce symptoms, we will knock it down with a milder form of chemotherapy. When it happens again, we'll knock it down in the same way." Wanting to encourage me, she continued, "The space in between episodes may be months or even a few years. Based on that prognosis, I needed to accept that future episodes were nearly guaranteed. The only unknowns were apparently when these future, unpredictable flareups would occur and what part of my body would be affected next.

In times when we are in great distress, we need to openly and honestly bring our fears to God Who can calm our anxious hearts. When we turn to Him, we discover that He is greater than our greatest fear. Our confidence in our ability to meet whatever challenges we face in life, including cancer, can not be primarily based on our own strength, for we are finite and subject to failing. Our confidence **must** be placed squarely and completely on the power of the Almighty God, the One who will not fail those who trust in Him. We can face the trial and get through the storm by the power of His Holy Spirit that dwells within the heart and mind of everyone who trusts in Him.

"He gives power to the weak, and to those who have no might, He increases strength."Isaiah 40:29 (NKJV)

"I waited patiently for God to help me; then He listened and heard my cry. He lifted me out of the pit of despair, out from the bog and the mire, and set my feet on a hard, firm path, and steadied me as I walked along." Psalm 40:1-2 (TLB)

When we're faced with a hard reality, there is often a significant disconnect between what the brain acknowledges as fact and what a heart is ready to receive. It can take awhile to fully process and even longer, sometimes **much** longer, to accept that truth and finally find peace. That was apparently why I struggled for several months to find peace with this third and most recent episode with my cancer. I needed to go beyond merely accepting the reality that my cancer, as a chronic disease subject to recurring flareups and subsequent treatments, would be with me for the remainder of my life. With God's help, I needed to come to see this from a different perspective. Although this latest prognosis was not what I had hoped for, nevertheless it was also a part of God's plan for me. By faith I needed to trust that He would ultimately work it out for good.

When I became a Christian as an eighteen year old teenager, I willingly surrendered my life to the Lord. It was a complete surrender, willingly choosing to exchange what I wanted and planned for my life for His plan. At the time, I couldn't possibly have known where He would lead me in the years ahead, but I was totally convinced that whatever He planned for me was **guaranteed** to be far better than whatever I might have planned for myself. As I look back now at the many decades that have passed since then, there have definitely been some challenges, some mountaintop experiences, as well as some deep valleys along the journey. I have also seen how God has not wasted those sorrows, those deep valley experiences, but was able to use them to help me mature and grow in "the fruits of The Spirit", thereby enriching my life and equipping me to be more of a blessing to others.

One of the ways that God encourages us in our trials is by the godly examples of others who have gone through their own "fiery trials", yet remained faithful and obedient to God. The apostle Paul was one of those incredible heroes of the faith. After his amazing conversion on the Road to Damascus, Paul's life was totally transformed from being one of the most feared persecutors of the early first century Church to become one of the greatest defenders of Christianity. He was used by God to preach the gospel far and wide, a missionary who planted and nurtured many churches among the Gentiles, and who authored many of the books in The New Testament. In a very honest and transparent manner, this amazing man of God recorded his prayers for healing from his own "thorn in the flesh" and how God answered his prayers.

> "There was given to me a thorn in the flesh, the messenger of Satan to buffet me, lest I should be exalted above measure. For this thing I besought the Lord thrice, that it might depart from me. And he said unto me, 'My grace is sufficient for thee; for my strength is made perfect in weakness. Most gladly therefore will I rather glory in my infirmities, that the power of Christ may rest upon me. Therefore I take pleasure in infirmities, in reproaches, in necessities, in persecutions, in distresses for Christ's sake: for when I am weak, then am I strong."
> 2 Corinthians 12:7b-10 (KJV)

God used this familiar passage to speak to me in a fresh way. Maybe it was the number three that caught my attention and struck a common chord, as I struggled to accept this third flareup of cancer, my personal "thorn in the flesh". It helped me to relate to Paul's personal struggle to understand and accept God's response to his three prayers for healing. I was both encouraged and challenged by Paul's example of a totally committed Christian who was struggling with a physical condition that he referred to as a "thorn in the flesh". He prayed three times that the Lord would heal him, by faith believing that with God all things are possible. The third time Paul prayed God answered his prayer, but it wasn't what Paul expected. God **didn't promise** that he would be healed, but that his "thorn in the flesh" was allowed for a higher purpose. Paul acknowledged that this affliction was useful to keep him grounded, not exalted in his own eyes because of his success, and daily depending on God. Healing wasn't promised, but Paul's perception and feeling about his infirmity completely changed when he understood that God's strength was made perfect in his weakness. After that revelation, everything changed for Paul. Understanding that his physical disability served a higher purpose, he gloried and even took pleasure in his infirmity, so that the power of Christ could rest upon him. When he was weak in the flesh, he was strong in the spirit.

Even though I would love to be completely healed, I also know that God may have a higher purpose for allowing my cancer to continue as it is. Whether He chooses to heal me or whether He chooses to sustain me as I am, I need to completely surrender the choice to Him and with all my heart pray as Jesus prayed to His Heavenly Father in the Garden of Gethsemane just hours before He was crucified,

"Nevertheless not my will, but thine, be done." Luke 22:42 (KJV)

Thirteen

Life Transforming Blessings of Cancer

"Whereas you do not know what will happen
tomorrow. For what is your life?
It is even a vapor that appears for a little time and
then vanishes away." James 4:14 (NKJV)

Nearly everyone who has ever experienced cancer will readily agree that cancer can impact and change our lives. Our familiar daily routine may be interrupted for weeks, months or even longer, while we persevere through chemotherapy, radiation, surgery, physical limitations or some combination of the above. It may also affect us financially, by limiting our ability to perform our jobs, as well as increasing our medical expenses. As unwelcome, disruptive and challenging as those changes can be, the good news is that cancer can also be used by God as a means of transforming our lives in some very significant and positive ways.

It's very typical for teens and younger adults to assume and plan their lives as if they are going to go on living forever, or at least to a "ripe old age". That may even be true for those of us who are well into our mid-life or senior years, especially if we have never before experienced an encounter with a serious health condition. At any age our perspective about life, our values, our priorities, goals we set and how we spend our time each day may be based on that assumption. Prior to cancer, I had always been blessed with exceptional health and assumed that I might live to be at least ninety as my mother had. Because of her excellent healthy life style, she didn't have any ongoing health issues nor needed to take any medication until she was eighty seven years of age.

That expectation changed during my third active episode with lymphoma, when I began thinking more about how much time I may still have left. Wondering if my life might actually be shorter than I expected, perhaps by several years. When I brought my concern to the Lord, praying that He would calm my anxious heart, His answer to my prayer was very clear and specific, "Don't be so concerned about how much time you may have left. Don't count the days, just make each day count." God's specific counsel to me that morning was so wise that it really changed my perspective and gave me peace and hope for my future. It greatly encouraged me and created within me a strong desire to redeem the time that I am given. After God changed my perspective about length of life vs. quality of life, by opening my mind and spirit and enabling me to see what's most important from His perspective, it made a difference in the goals I set each year, as well as my things-to-do list for each day. With a new awareness that each day we're given is a gift from God, I now want to use the time and opportunities that God gives me to glorify Him and to be a blessing to others.

> "Teach us to number our days and recognize how
> few they are; help us to spend them as we should."
> Psalm 90:12 (TLB)

Far too often it's very convenient for us to keep putting off making some of life's most important decisions. It's just more convenient to choose, instead, to defer making those decisions until another day. As convenient as that may be at the moment, repeatedly deferring making the most critical decisions of our lives may have a tragic consequence, since we aren't guaranteed that we will actually be granted another day of life. Being diagnosed with cancer can definitely shake up our pattern of complacency and procrastination and motivate us to begin seriously considering our own mortality, perhaps for the first time. It's one thing for us to acknowledge that truth in a general way, but cancer has a way of moving the matter from "the back burner" to "the front burner" of our minds with a new level of urgency. It compels us to take a broad look back at our lives and ask ourselves some very important questions:

> How has my life mattered up until now?
> How have I used the talents, resources and opportunities God has given me?
> Have I invested enough time with my family, nurturing them in the ways of the Lord or have I spent it on lesser things.
> How have I invested my life in the work of the Lord, in ways that make a difference in the lives of others for eternity?

If we are being honest with ourselves, the answers will open our eyes to see some serious changes that we need to make in our lives. So it is that God can use cancer to get our attention, enable us to see the need to turn our lives around and then point us in a new direction ... while there is still time.

Another area of our lives that cancer can dramatically change is in our priorities. I know of a man who was a rising star on the corporate ladder of a major corporation. Shortly after being promoted to a regional five state sales manager, he said confidently, "My next step will be vice president." He was receiving the recognition and rewards of being a dedicated and successful employee and looked forward to a very promising future with his company. Unfortunately, about a year after his promotion he was diagnosed with an advanced case of metastatic cancer, with a prognosis of possibly three to four years to live. Because of the severe pain he was in, he was unable to work for the next six months; and when he finally did return to work, it was only on a very limited part time basis. His plans and expectations for a promising career had been dramatically changed by cancer, but so had his priorities. When he considered the limited time that he might have left, he wisely decided to invest those remaining years in his pre-teen son. Cancer helped him to see that investing time with his young son was a higher priority and of greater value than gaining success, with all the perks that come with it in the corporate world.

In addition to motivating us to make each day count and resetting our priorities, cancer can also be used by God to get our attention and encourage us to make the most life transforming change of all. A diagnosis of advanced cancer can force some patients, especially those with a limited prognosis, to ask themselves the questions that they have intentionally avoided asking until now, "When I die, what will happen to me? Where will I spend eternity? I hope it's heaven, but how can I know **for sure** that I am going to be there?" How they respond will make the difference between being eternally saved or lost. Spending eternity in heaven or hell.

My father was one example of a man whose life was radically transformed by advanced cancer. Growing up in the heart of Chicago during the Great Depression years, he developed a tough demeanor, probably as a defensive measure to stand up to the street gangs of that day. Fiercely independent, he lived nearly sixty years of his life feeling like he didn't need help from anyone, not even God. He essentially considered himself to be a self-made man, who credited his success in life to his own intelligence, strength, ability and hard work. As long as life was good, he was satisfied with all he had accomplished on his own. After I became a Christian, I was concerned about my Dad's salvation. I prayed for him and tried to share the gospel with him for sixteen years, but he showed no apparent interest. God was able to use advanced cancer as a means of motivating him to get serious about where he would spend eternity. Within just a matter of a few weeks after he was diagnosed, my dad's demeanor changed from being fiercely proud and independent to being broken in spirit, from fearless and afraid of no one to being fearful and anxious. The turning point for my dad came when I visited him in the hospital and, for the first time, he told me he'd been praying about how he could know for sure that he was saved. Two days later my pastor went down to the veteran's hospital in Chicago and led him to Jesus Christ as his savior. In the remaining three weeks of his life, my dad's uncertainty and fear about his eternal future was totally gone. With total peace, he passed from this life into the very presence of the living God, Who loved him, saved him and with open arms welcomed him home.

There is no greater question that we all need to ask ourselves than, "Where will I spend eternity?" This life we are living now is really quite temporary when compared to eternity. What an incredible difference it makes for you and for me to have complete assurance that when the time comes, the time appointed by God before we were born when we pass from this life, we will be met at heaven's door by an angelic escort and welcomed into our heavenly home.

God loves us and has provided a way for us to have that confident assurance of eternal life through the sacrificial death, burial and resurrection of His only Son, Jesus. We can learn about His plan, as recorded in His Word, the Holy Bible:

1. **The first step is to acknowledge that we have sinned.** No matter how good we are, or think we are, none of us can honestly say that we have **never** sinned.

    "For all have sinned and fall short of the glory of God." Romans 3:23 (NKJV)

    "If we say that we have no sin, we deceive ourselves, and the truth is not in us."

"If we say that we have not sinned, we make (God) a liar, and His word is not in us." I John 1:8,10 (NKJV)

2. **The just penalty for our sins is eternal death**, but the good news is that God has provided a perfect, sinless substitute to pay for our sins through the death of His Son, Jesus Christ.

   "If we confess our sins, he is faithful and just to forgive us our sins, and to cleanse us from all unrighteousness." I John 1:9 (KJV)

   "For the wages of sin is death, but the gift of God is eternal life in Christ Jesus our Lord." Romans 6:23 (NKJV)

   "For whoever calls on the name of the Lord shall be saved." Romans 10:13 (NKJV)

3. **Salvation is a gift of God.** We don't deserve it, and we can't earn it by our good works. It's **all** by God's mercy and grace and Jesus' sacrifice.

   "For by grace you have been saved through faith, and that not of yourselves; it is the gift of God, not of works, lest anyone should boast." Ephesians 2:8-9 (NKJV)

4. **Believe that Jesus Christ is The Holy Son of God**, Who was crucified for our sins and has risen from the dead.

   "For God so loved the world, that he gave His only begotten Son, that whosoever believeth in Him should not perish, but have everlasting life." John 3:16 (KJV)

"As many as received (Jesus), to them He gave the right to become children of God, to those who believe in His name." John 1:10 (NKJV)

5. **Share the blessing, the Good News, with others**. Romans 10:9-10 (NKJV)

"That if you confess with your mouth the Lord Jesus and believe in your heart that God has raised Him from the dead, you will be saved. For with the heart one believes unto righteousness, and with the mouth confession is made unto salvation."

When you consider what's at stake, have you made that all important decision to receive the gift of eternal life that God offers to you: the unmerited forgiveness of your sins through the death and resurrection of His Son, Jesus Christ; to receive Him as your Savior and Lord; and commit to follow and serve Him for the rest of your life?

If you have made that most important decision of your life,
Congratulations and
welcome to the family of God.

Fourteen

Strive to Finish Well

I have fought a good fight, I have finished
my course, I have kept the faith:
henceforth there is laid up for me a crown
of righteousness, which the Lord,
the righteous judge, shall give me at that day: and not to me only,
but unto all them also that love his
appearing. 2 Timothy 4:7-8 (KJV)

My family recently came together to celebrate my birthday, a special milestone birthday to mark another decade of my life. Each passing year, when one more candle adorns the top of my birthday cake, serves as an annual reminder that God has been faithful to me in the year ending and the remaining years that He has planned for me are fewer. That motivates me to redeem the time I am given and strive through the power of the Holy Spirit to finish well.

It's important for each of us to strive to finish well in our journey of life. As we get older, we are more inclined to look back and reflect on what we have accomplished so far. Even when with God's help we have accomplished many things, what we may be most remembered for, after we are gone, is how we finished the race. So what exactly do we need to consider that will help us to finish our life's journey with excellence?

Finishing well involves putting our affairs in order. Pertaining to health, it means completing both a Healthcare Power of Attorney and a Living Will. A Healthcare Power of Attorney allows you to designate someone that you trust to make decisions related to your healthcare if you are unable to. A Living Will indicates what your wishes are pertaining to end of life care. Your primary physician will often be able to supply both forms to you without charge and assist you with completing them if you need help. It's usually advisable to inform your adult children about your wishes and where these important documents are kept.

When it comes to financial matters, putting our affairs in order includes executing (completing) a will and/or a trust. Both are legal documents, best prepared with the help of an attorney. While both can indicate who you wish to receive your assets at the time of your passing, there are some important differences. A will is a public document and effective only after your passing, which in some cases can be costly and take months or longer to fully execute your wishes for your estate. A trust, on the other hand, is a private document that can be used to manage your assets while you live, and can also allow someone else that you elect to manage your assets on your behalf if you are unable. If you are tempted to avoid making the time to set up these important documents because 1) the process may seem a little intimidating, or 2) you may believe that a will or a trust is just for the rich and famous, there's something you need to know. For those who neglect to set up either a will or a trust while they are living and of a sound mind, the state you reside in will decide who inherits your assets at the time of your death. Beside the length of time your estate could be tied up in court, whatever you leave behind may not even be passed onto the loved ones or ministries that you would have chosen.

Moving on from the weightier side of life, there is one aspect of finishing well that can actually be creative, fun, and well worth the time and effort. It's about writing your legacy story, the story of your life and the lives of those who preceded you. It's a great way to preserve and pass on to your family somethings about your family lineage. Where your ancestors originally came from, what they accomplished and how they got through challenging times like The Great Depression and World War II years. You can share interesting stories that were passed on to you by your parents and grandparents about the generations that preceded them. This is a perfect opportunity to honor the everyday heroes in your family line. Of course, you will also want to include your own memories about growing up, and the significant events of your life. I would especially encourage you to share your personal faith journey, so that your children, grandchildren and generations to come will be encouraged to trust in the Lord and be faithful to Him throughout their lifetime. The process can be as simple as handwriting it down on a few sheets of paper, or you may prefer to use one of those books that prompt our memories by asking questions and allows space to write down our answers. If you feel really ambitious, you can go further and forward your manuscript to a self-publishing company, that will guide you step by step through the process of transforming your manuscript into a real, professional quality book. Think of yourself as being the custodian of your personal and your family's history. If we don't take the time to preserve it, it may soon be forgotten after we are gone.

Another way to finish well that will really bless your loved ones is to write a note or letter to each one, to be opened after your passing. You can tell them how much you love them, how much you value them and your relationship, and how you appreciate the specific ways that they reached out to help and encourage you. You may go on to bless them like the patriarchs did in the bible, by encouraging them to stay true to the Lord throughout their lifetime. Of all the things you may leave them one day as an inheritance, this may be the one thing that will be the most appreciated and valued.

When cancer strikes, it can even impact our ability to continue to fulfill our role as a ministry leader. For the past nine years, I have had the privilege to serve in my church as a co-facilitator of a support group for widows. I have loved serving the Lord in this way, but dealing with cancer during the past three years has limited my ability to be present at many of the meetings. The Lord has used this to teach me an important principle about finishing well in the area of ministry. One of the essential roles of a ministry leader **must** be to recruit and prepare the person that the Lord has selected who will eventually succeed them. It's the only way that a ministry can continue when the current leader needs to step down. We need to begin by asking the Lord to guide us to the right person(s); and then be diligent about mentoring and preparing them, so that they will be ready to step up when the time comes for us to step down. The bible gives us several examples of godly leaders who were mindful about preparing the one(s) that God had chosen to succeed them. When the appointed time came and their work on earth was done, they were able to "pass on the torch" to their successor(s) and finished well. Moses mentored and trained Joshua for forty years as they lead the nation of Israel through the wilderness. Elijah handed his cloak to Elisha just before he was transported by a chariot of fire to heaven. The apostle Paul mentored Timothy, who he described as "a true son in the faith". 1 Timothy 1:2 (NKJV). Jesus closely mentored and trained his twelve disciples for three years. One of the last things He did before ascending back to His Father in heaven was to instruct His disciples to follow His example and continue to share the gospel and make disciples after He was gone.

> "Therefore go and make disciples in all the nations, baptizing them into the name of the Father and of the Son and of the Holy Spirit, and then teach these new disciples to obey all the commands I have given you; and be sure of this - that I am with you always, even to the end of the world." Matthew 28:19-20 (TLB)

When we aren't able to continue leading, or even participating on a regular basis, a ministry that we've loved, it may leave us for awhile with a feeling of sadness. That's certainly understandable, because it is a kind of loss; and any kind of loss is usually coupled with some feelings of grief. God understands those feelings and has helped me when I've gone through some major life changes by giving me a new perspective. The ending of one thing is often coupled with the beginning of another. That "new beginning" perspective encourages me, because it helps me to focus more on new beginnings and opportunities rather than on what's ending. Even if we are confined to our homes much of the time, that means that we have more time to develop a ministry of prayer. I like to pray for a different group of people every day of the week, i.e. family, friends, my church and other ministries, our nation and our leaders. It's helpful to keep a prayer journal, listing who you prayed for and how your prayers were answered. We can also develop a ministry of encouragement. By a phone call or a note, we can let others know we are thinking of them and praying for them. You can even encourage those who come into your home, either to visit with you or provide some form of at home care. You will probably find that God will provide many opportunities for you to share your own testimony with others, the story of how God worked in your life and how He can help them too.

> "So ever since we first heard about you, we have kept on praying and asking God to help you understand what he wants you to do; asking Him to make you wise about spiritual things; and asking that the way you live will always please the Lord and honor him, so that you will always be doing good, kind things for others, while all the time you are learning to know God better and better." Colossians 1:9-10 (TLB)

For Christians, we should strive to finish well; because we

represent our Heavenly Father to a world that is asking, "What difference does it make to be a Christian? Some who ask are skeptical and doubting. Some feel self-sufficient and have no need to make a change. But some are sincere, wanting to know if there's more to life than they are experiencing. When we go through cancer or some other serious illness, we have the opportunity to demonstrate to those around us that **it truly makes all the difference in the world**. By the power of the Holy Spirit that dwells within the heart and life of every believer, we can endure the trial with courage, hope and the peace that passes understanding that only God can supply. God may use your example and testimony of being faithful under fiery trials to encourage someone else who is going through their own trial, possibly their own time with cancer, to turn to Him and find hope and peace.

> "Quietly trust yourself to Christ your Lord, and if anybody asks why you believe as you do, be ready to tell him, and do it in a gentle and respectful way."
> I Peter 3:15 (TLB)

> "Let your light so shine before men, that they may see your good works, and glorify your Father which is in heaven." Matthew 5:16 (KJV)

Finally, the unidentified author of the book of Hebrews in the New Testament describes a Christian as a runner in the Race of Life. As a runner, he encourages us to continue to stay the course that God has planned for us and not quit before we get to the finish line. He further challenges and encourages us by reminding us that we are not alone in the race.

> "Therefore we also, since we are surrounded by so great a cloud of witnesses, let us lay aside every weight, and the sin which so easily ensnares us, and

let us run with endurance the race that is set before us, looking unto Jesus, the author and finisher of our faith, who for the joy that was set before Him endured the cross, despising the shame, and has sat down at the right hand of the throne of God." Hebrews 12:1-2 (NKJV)

"And let us not get tired of doing what is right, for after a while we will reap a harvest of blessing if we don't get discouraged and give up." Galatians 6:9 (TLB)

In any race, runners are remembered primarily by how they finished the race, more than how they started out or ran the course. Few are remembered or received any recognition or reward who didn't finish the race and dropped out. Some Christian leaders served the Lord for many years, even decades. Through hard work and their commitment to the Lord, God blessed their work. Sadly, there came a time when they yielded to temptation, possibly pride from their success or from some other sin that entangled them, and in shame wound up either choosing to, or were forced to, drop out of the very ministry they may have even started.

"In a race everyone runs, but only one person gets first prize. So run your race to win. To win the contest you must deny yourselves many things that would keep you from doing your best. An athlete goes to all this trouble just to win a blue ribbon or a silver cup, but we do it for a heavenly reward that never disappears. So I run straight to the goal with purpose in every step. I fight to win." 1 Corinthians 9:24-26 (TLB)

"But none of these things move me; nor do I count my life dear to myself, so that I may finish my race with joy, and the ministry which I received from the Lord Jesus, to testify to the gospel of the grace of God." Acts 20:24 (NKJV)

So run your race with excellence, striving
to finish well and win the prize.

Fifteen

The Best is Yet to Come

For this world is not our home; we are looking forward to
our everlasting home in heaven. Hebrews 13:14 (TLB)

Very early in my journey through cancer my mind started filling
with questions. I felt that the more I learned and understood
about my new disease, Non-Hodgkins Lymphoma, the better I
could prepare myself for what may lie ahead of me. What would
the radiation treatments be like? Would the rapidly developing
symptoms caused by the large tumor in my neck completely be
resolved? How long would it take? My oncologist tried to help me
set realistic expectations at our first appointment, by explaining that
cancer just isn't that predictable. He didn't offer any 100 percent
guarantees, nor could he, about how the treatments would affect
me or what the outcome would be after treatment. From then on, I
understood that when it comes to cancer, or life itself, there are no
guarantees.

Without guarantees, bigger questions seemed to naturally follow.
If God chooses not to heal me and the end of my life on earth is
nearer, possibly much nearer than I had thought, what would that
be like? What might I experience at the moment when I will pass on
from this life? I was so thankful to know that my Heavenly Father,

the One who knows my heart and mind, knows my every anxious thought and hears every unspoken word, loves me and understands.

As I wrestled with these ultimate questions about life and death, the Lord used at least three things to encourage my heart and bring me hope and peace. I was encouraged by the amazing example of my cousin, Pat Czerkies, in her battle with breast cancer over several years. Soon after her diagnosis, Pat became a Christian through a neighborhood bible study group that she and her husband, Ted, hosted in their home. She had a radiant testimony to all that knew her, choosing to use her time to bless others and glorify God. When I called her one day to see how she was doing, she said, "I can't talk very long right now. I am baking cookies with my granddaughter." Pat chose to focus on life and the opportunities she had to invest her life in the people nearest and dearest to her. Farther along in her journey, I went to visit her again. This time I couldn't help but notice that, in spite of all she was going through, she seemed to have an incredible peace and joy. When I commended her for having such peace, she replied, "Joyce, I look at it this way. If the Lord chooses to heal me of this cancer and lets me live long enough to see my grandchildren grow up, marry and eventually see their children, I win. If, on the other hand, He doesn't heal me, and I go to be with Him in heaven, I win. Either way, it's a 'win-win' situation. I can't lose." Pat's "win-win" perspective was truly amazing and helped to encourage others, especially other cancer patients she met, to see their own health challenges with a new perspective.

There was an incredible sense of peace in confidently knowing that after I die my next destination would be heaven. I tried to imagine what I might experience in that moment of time when I pass on from my present mortal life to begin experiencing a new kind of life, immortal life, a life that will continue to go on forever, for all eternity with the Lord. I believe that it's the soul that gives life to the body. At the moment of death, only the body dies. Our immortal soul, the thing that gave life to the body, will continue to go on living, probably experiencing life in an even larger sense.

I remembered trying to explain this phenomenon to the Hospice chaplain, who came in to sit with me for awhile after my mother died. "My mother isn't dead. Only her body has died. She's probably more alive now than she's ever been before."

I tried to imagine who might be there in heaven to greet and welcome me when I arrive. I thought of it being like going back home again for a wonderful family reunion. Experiencing the joy of being together again with those who have gone on before me and will be there to greet me when I arrive. Even greater than being with loved ones again, Jesus Himself will be there to welcome me home.

> "Jesus said, "In My Father's house are many mansions; if it were not so, I would have told you. I go to prepare a place for you. And if I go and prepare a place for you, I will come again and receive you to Myself; that where I am, there you may be also."
> John 14:2-3 (NKJV)

What will heaven look like? The Apostle Paul described the magnificence of heaven. Its glory and its beauty going beyond anything that we can possibly imagine or compare it to. He wrote in his letter to the church at Corinth:

> "This is what is meant by the Scriptures which say that no mere man has ever seen, heard, or even imagined what wonderful things God has ready for those who love the Lord." I Corinthians 2:9 (TLB)

I went on and tried to imagine what it would be like to pass through the Pearly Gates of heaven and proceed to enter into the Throne Room, into the very presence of the Almighty God and see Him face to face for the first time. The bible gives us a preview of heaven through the eye witness testimony of a few who were privileged to have a vision of heaven and recorded it before they died:

The prophet Isaiah's vision of heaven is recorded in the Old Testament.

> "In the year that King Uzziah died, I saw the Lord sitting on a throne, high and lifted up, and the train of His robe filled the temple. Above it stood seraphim; each one had six wings: with two he covered his face, with two he covered his feet, and with two he flew. And one cried to another and said, 'Holy, holy, holy is the Lord of hosts; the whole earth is full of His glory.'" Isaiah 6:1-3 (NKJV)

In the New Testament book of Revelation, the apostle John wrote extensively about his vision of heaven, while he was exiled for his faith on the Isle of Patmos.

> "And instantly I was in spirit there in heaven and saw - oh, the glory of it! - a throne and someone sitting on it! Great bursts of light flashed forth from him as from a glittering diamond or from a shining ruby, and a rainbow glowing like an emerald encircled His throne." Revelation 4:2-3 (TLB)

> "After this I heard the shouting of a vast crowd in heaven, 'Hallelujah! Praise the Lord! Salvation is from our God. Honor and authority belong to Him alone.'" Revelation 19:1 (TLB)

God also gave the apostle John a vision of a future time, a time when our present world would pass away and be replaced by a "new earth."

> "Then I saw a new earth (with no oceans!) and a new sky, for the present earth and sky had disappeared.

And I, John, saw the Holy City, the new Jerusalem, coming down from God out of heaven. It was a glorious sight, beautiful as a bride at her wedding. I heard a shout from the throne saying, 'Look, the home of God is now among men, and he will live with them and they will be His people; yes, God himself will be among them. He will wipe away all tears from their eyes, and there shall be no more death, nor sorrow, nor crying, nor pain. All of that has gone forever.'" Revelation 21:1-4 (TLB)

"And the city has no need of sun or moon to light it, for the glory of God and of the Lamb illuminate it." Revelation 21:23 (TLB)

Based on what has been written and carefully preserved for millennia by God Himself, I could only imagine what is yet to come will bring incredible comfort and ultimate joy. **A time when all our tears will be wiped away; and there will be no more death, nor sorrow, nor crying, nor pain. All that will be gone forever!!** In a moment I will be welcomed by a heavenly escort and ushered into a place that goes beyond any words that can adequately describe the glory and beauty of it. I will enter into the very presence of the living, eternal God and see Him high and lifted up upon His throne. I will hear the angels surrounding the throne, who will join in with the multitude who've put their trust in Christ, and singing their praises. A future time will come when I will look upward and see the New Jerusalem, descending from on high, glorious and radiant beyond compare; it will be a time of perfect peace, no more sin, no more wars, no more cancer, or global pandemics.

The more I thought about what's yet to come, the more excited I became. I thought if God has chosen not to heal my cancer, if His plan is to bring me into His presence sooner than I had expected, I will finally get to see in person what I can only imagine now. My former anxiety about the possibility of dying sooner than I expected was turned into eager anticipation. Moving way beyond feeling like "Woe is me" to "WOW!!" What lay ahead of me was so awesome that I felt that I could hardly wait. If, on the other hand, God has chosen to give me additional years to remain on earth, I want to spend that gift of time to be a blessing to others and bring glory to Him.

The apostle Paul apparently had the same conflict of feelings about whether it is better to live or to die and wrote about it in his letter to the church at Phillipi:

> "If living will give me more opportunities to win people to Christ, then I really don't know which is better, to live or die. Sometimes I want to live, and at other times I don't, for I long to go and be with Christ. How much happier for me than being here. But the fact is that I can be of more help to you by staying." Philippians 1:22-24 (TLB)

For all those who have placed their trust in Christ, and Christ alone to save them from their sins, there is peace and joy in knowing that the best is yet to come. Until that time, Jesus warned his disciples and us, that as long as we are in this world we **will** go through difficult times and our mortal bodies **will be** vulnerable to diseases like cancer. So we can persevere through these trials, when we remember that our "troubles will soon be over, but the joys to come will last forever."

> "That is why we never give up. Though our bodies are dying, our inner strength in the Lord is growing every day. These troubles and sufferings of ours are, after all, quite small and won't last very long. Yet this short time of distress will result in God's richest blessing upon us forever and ever! So we do not look

at what we can see right now, the troubles all around us, but we look forward to the joys in heaven we have not yet seen. The troubles will soon be over, but the joys to come will last forever." II Corinthians 4:16-18 (TLB)

Finally, we have God's promises that the best of yet to come.
"For I consider that the sufferings of this present time are not worthy to be compared with the glory which shall be revealed in us."Romans 8:18 (NKJV)

"Everyone who conquers will inherit all these blessings, and I will be his God and he will be my son."Revelation 21:7 (TLB)

So we need to run the race, keeping our eye on the goal, and strive with the power of the Holy Spirit to finish well the course that God has planned for you and for me. We can have the confidence that whatever you and I are going through now, or may yet lie ahead of us,

it will be worth it all when we see Jesus.

Sixteen

God's Love Never Fails

Yet in all these things we are more than
conquerors through Him who loved us.
For I am persuaded that neither death nor life,
nor angels nor principalities nor powers,
nor things present nor things to come, nor height
nor depth, nor any other created thing,
shall be able to separate us from the love of
God which is in Christ Jesus our Lord.
Romans 8:37-39 (NKJV)

For the past three years, I've been walking through this ongoing journey called cancer. The path that I am still traveling has sometimes lead me through the valley with dark shadows, but there were other times when the same path has lead me upward, as I lifted my eyes unto my Lord, my source of help and strength. As I ascended the path the Good Shepherd was leading me through, the clouds parted, the light of the sun broke through, and ominous shadows of fear and despair were left far below. When I reached the pinnacle of my journey, my spirit lifted as I remembered the visions of great men of faith, who were privileged to see and record the blessings to come for me and for every believer who places their trust in Him, and in Him alone, for salvation. Based on their description, I could almost see the most indescribably beautiful and glorious panoramic view from the mountaintop.

Having been to the top of the mountain has helped me to see it all now more clearly from God's perspective. As difficult and challenging as the journey has been at times, it was part of His divine plan and purpose for my life. He doesn't want me to waste the struggle, the sighs, or tears shed, but desires for me to use what I have learned from the journey to encourage others in their valley times and bring even more glory and honor to Him for His abiding presence, faithfulness, and love.

The journey with cancer has definitely been a challenging experience, but God used each challenge that I experienced to teach me so many lessons. Lessons that have served His ultimate purpose to enrich my life, teaching me things I might not have learned as well, or not at all, apart from traveling through this journey. God used cancer to help me appreciate so many everyday, ordinary blessings that, prior to cancer, I had failed to fully appreciate: the blessing of being able to use my voice to speak and to join with other believers in singing praises to our God; for physical strength and ability to simply rise up in the morning and lay down every night without help; and for the blessing of a good night's sleep uninterrupted by pain. Even though pain is never something we typically desire or wish for, I learned that pain can often be an unwelcome blessing in disguise, intended to alert us that something is going on within us that needs to be checked out, before it gets worse. When I wondered if, because of cancer, my days and years might be more limited than I had planned or expected, God encouraged me not to count the days, but to make each day count. I have learned to value each day that I am given as a fleeting and irreplaceable gift from God, which has motivated me to redeem the time I'm given and daily conform my priorities and things I plan to do with that fresh awareness in mind. By my third episode with lymphoma, I finally learned why the Divine Creator of the universe and everything in it, including our bodies, knows us better than we do and encourages us to cultivate a healthy lifestyle of balancing time for work with time for rest, responsibility with recreation, and time for others with time to be alone with God.

When cancer strikes close to home, or we experience some other type of adversity, many begin to question: Why do bad things happen to good people?; If God is really so loving and so good, why this? Why me? Why now? While we may not know, nor fully understand, the answers to those questions until we enter into His holy presence one day, I have seen many evidences of God's love during my own journey. When my strength failed and I needed help, God in His foreknowledge knew what would happen long before I knew and had already positioned others who were available and willing to care for me when the time came. When I needed a fresh daily infusion of divine hope, He assured me that He would faithfully supply my needs for each day. I am totally confident that He was never too busy to hear my earnest prayers and know my heart. When I was discouraged and tears began to fall, He didn't scold me for doubting His goodness or for being weak of faith. Instead He warmly welcomed me to come to Him just as I am, as a hurting child comes to a loving father, surrounded me with a strong sense of His holy presence, and comforted me. Through it all, He gave me a peace that passes understanding and an assurance that He would never leave me nor forsake me and would be with me throughout the journey.

God may also allow His children to be touched by cancer or some other disease or affliction to test our faith. These "fiery trials" of adversity are not intended to destroy us but to refine us, as gold is of greater value after it has been refined and purified by fire.

I have also discovered that every challenge we face, every trial we endure, every loss we suffer creates opportunities for God to work in us and then through us. The greater the challenge, the greater the opportunity. By them, He equips us with new knowledge and a spirit of compassion for others who are going through a similar trial.

He may then commission us to go where we might not otherwise have planned or chosen to go, so that He could use us, as His ambassadors, to minister to and encourage other patients that we might meet there.

Though healing was never promised, I am very thankful that my condition is currently described as being stable. I have been cautiously advised to be prepared that it may become active again from time to time, possibly in a new area and/or with a new set of symptoms. If and when that happens, I have even more reasons now than ever before, because of all that God has taught me in this journey through cancer, to be confident that He, Who has never failed me before, will not fail me then and will continue to be with me and help me to finish well in the race of life. And when this life is past, I have God's promise that the best is yet to come.

Until that divinely appointed day and time comes, when I am welcomed and invited to enter into the very presence of my Heavenly Father, I am encouraged by Psalm 23:1-4, 6 (NKJV) in my ongoing journey through this valley.

"The Lord is my shepherd: I shall not want.
He makes me to lie down in green pastures;
He leads me beside the still waters. He restores my soul;
He leads me in the paths of righteousness for His name's sake.
Yea, though I walk through the valley of the shadow of death,
I will fear no evil; for You are with me."

"Surely goodness and mercy shall follow
me all the days of my life; and
(when this life is over) I will dwell in the
house of the Lord forever."

The best is yet to come!

CPSIA information can be obtained
at www.ICGtesting.com
Printed in the USA
BVHW030238040321
601702BV00019B/133